COME TO THE ALTAR

WORSHIPPING GOD WITH YOUR WHOLE HEART

FR. MIKE SCHMITZ

ASCENSION

West Chester, Pennsylvania

Excerpts from the English translation of the *Catechism of the Catholic Church* for use in the United States of America © 1994, 1997 by the United States Catholic Conference, Inc.–Libreria Editrice Vaticana. Used by permission. All rights reserved.

Unless otherwise noted, Scripture passages are from the Revised Standard Version–Second Catholic Edition © 2006 by the Division of Christian Education of the National Council of the Churches of Christ in the United States of America. Used by permission. All rights reserved.

Ascension
PO Box 1990
West Chester, PA 19380
1-800-376-0520

ascensionpress.com
Cover design: James Kegley

Printed in the United States of America
23 24 25 26 27 5 4 3 2 1

ISBN 978-1-954882-22-5 (trade book)
ISBN 978-1-954882-23-2 (e-book)

CONTENTS

WELCOME TO THE SUNDAY HOMILIES WITH FR. MIKE SCHMITZ COLLECTION

Each booklet in this series has been created to invite Catholics to grow closer to God through reflections from Fr. Mike.

These booklets are short and relatable, with features that will help you apply what you read to your own life.

Quotes and Bible verses throughout the booklets will help you zero in on the key points.

Questions after each section prompt you to reflect and help you to dive deeper into the topic being presented. We recommend that you pray or journal with these questions as you make connections to your everyday life. (They also make great prompts for small group discussion, while keeping in mind that not everyone in your group may feel comfortable answering those of a more personal nature.)

Meditations are provided after each reflection to help you take the topic directly into prayer. We recommend setting aside some time after each chapter to read the meditation and pray or journal with it.

Each reflection ends with a challenge to put what you have learned into action. These challenges invite you to enter into prayer, serve others, make a resolution for the week, and more.

It is our sincere hope **The Sunday Homilies with Fr. Mike Schmitz Collection** helps you along the way in your journey toward holiness. May God bless you!

*Note: This booklet is adapted from homilies given by Fr. Mike Schmitz.

CHAPTER 1

WHERE IS YOUR ALTAR?

There are two kinds of people who become fans of something: those who want to actually do it themselves, and those who want to watch someone else do it. There are those who play football, and others who watch them play. There are those who play music, and those who want to listen to others play it well.

Recently, some friends of mine got tickets to a concert. The tickets were really hard to get—a team of multiple people had to watch their computers all day in order to get two tickets. I asked, "You know all the songs already. You can just listen online. Why did you make such a huge effort to get tickets?" The answer was, "I just want to be there."

That makes sense. We just want to be at a concert or be at the game. As human beings, just being somewhere is valuable sometimes.

At the same time, even if we are the kind of fans who just watch a ballgame or concert, we still want to be part of the action. If we had the chance and the ability, all of us would prefer not just to observe but to participate, to be part of something great. This desire is built into us.

I'll admit that in every concert I've ever been to, I always think that if one of their singers drops out, I'll be the person to help them, because I want to be part of it. Now you might say I just have a highly inflated opinion of myself. But seriously, there's a sense of not just wanting to be there but wanting to do something.

The crazy thing is that we settle. We settle for watching other people do great things. We are entertained by seeing them doing these great things. It doesn't cost us anything. This is not a bad thing in itself, but often it *is* settling.

The primary thing we're called to do is to love.

Both being present and doing things are good. We need to understand this, because we get into error when we emphasize one to the exclusion of the other. There are people who are overworked, who are all about doing, doing, doing. They have to be reminded that we're not "human doings," we're human beings. At the same time, as human beings, God made us to do things.

The biggest thing God made us for is at the heart of our identity. It's actually the heart of his identity. The biggest thing God made us to do is to love. We can experience love, and that is a gift, but to choose to love is at the core of who we are. The primary thing we're called to do is to love.

THE GREATEST COMMANDMENT

In the Gospel of Matthew, we see a lawyer approached Jesus with an important question. I think that unlike some of the Pharisees, who often were trying to ensnare Jesus in some kind of trap, this was a genuine guy who wanted to know the answer to a genuine question. He asked, "Teacher, which is the great commandment in the law?" (Matthew 22:36). He wanted to know how he could love God more. The answer is this: Jesus told him that the greatest commandment is, "You shall love the Lord your God with all your heart, and with all your soul, and with all your mind" (Matthew 22:37).

THE GREATEST COMMANDMENT

"But when the Pharisees heard that he had silenced the Sadducees, they came together. And one of them, a lawyer, asked him a question, to test him. 'Teacher, which is the great commandment in the law?' And he said to him, 'You shall love the Lord your God with all your heart, and with all your soul, and with all your mind. This is the great and first commandment. And a second is like it, You shall love your neighbor as yourself. On these two commandments depend all the law and the prophets'" (Matthew 22:34–40).

Now, I am guessing that almost all of us could say that we know the greatest commandment. Knowing it is easy. But our next question to Jesus is harder: "How do we do that, Lord?" How does anyone love God?

When it comes to loving each other, that is one thing. We know that the definition of love is to "will the good" of another—to give them what is good, what they need. But God doesn't *need* anything. God is goodness itself. He doesn't need us at all. If I will God's good, I can't add to his goodness. So how do we will the good of the One who is the source of all good? How can we truly love God?

We're made to love, but how do we do it when it comes to God?

Scripture reveals that there are three ways we can actually love God.

The first way is something St. John talks about (see 1 John 4:20–21). He says we can know we love God if we care for the people around us, including those who need our love, attention, or help. We love God by loving our brother or sister.

We love God when we worship him.

The second way we love God is by obeying him. As Jesus says, "If you love me, you will keep my commandments" (John 14:15). We can't claim to love God and not obey his commandments. We love God through obedience to his commandments, and so if I am ever questioning if I really love God enough, I have to look at how I am acting, not how I am feeling. I need to look at whether I am choosing to obey him.

So, I can love God by willing the good of the people around me who need love. I can love God by obeying him. And the third way I can love God is an extension of obeying him. We love God when we worship him as he has asked us to worship him, and this is key. We love the Lord our God with everything we have and everything we are through obedience and worship.

COME TO THE ALTAR

The problem for us as Catholics is that we can "settle" when we go to Mass. We are called to love God, and we love God by worshipping him. But so often, we come to Mass and just watch.

According to recent surveys, Mass attendance in the United States is at an all-time low. Only 17 percent of American Catholics attend Mass regularly.[1] And many of us who do show up, do it wrong. Now, I know you may be thinking, "But Father, I know all the 'moves'—when to stand, when to sit, and what to say." Well, that's wonderful. Keep it up. But that is just "showing up" at Mass; it is settling for just watching.

Let's be clear: We were not created to just watch the Mass. We were not baptized and redeemed by Jesus to just *watch* the priest pray his prayers, hear the readings, and listen to the music. But many of us have become a people of God who are willing simply to watch worship.

If we as Catholics don't know how to worship, we don't know what we have been made for. We don't know how to love God as he has called us to love him.

Every one of us is called to worship, and we worship at the altar. So we need to talk about what an altar is and what it has to do with loving God.

THE ALTAR OF SACRIFICE

In response to Satan's temptations in the wilderness, Jesus says, "It is written, 'You shall worship the Lord your God, and him only shall you serve'" (Luke 4:8). The word "serve" here in the original Greek is *latria*, which means "adore" or "worship." We are to worship and serve God alone.

This is why the heart of the Christian Faith is not just a list of teachings— it is not just about *what* we believe but *who* we believe in. As we proclaim in the Nicene Creed, "I believe in one God, the Father almighty, maker of heaven and earth … I believe in one Lord Jesus Christ, the Only Begotten Son of God … I believe in the Holy Spirit, the Lord, the giver of life." We let everyone know and remind ourselves *who* we are worshipping in the Mass: the triune God—Father, Son, and Holy Spirit.

How do we love God? By loving others and by obeying and worshipping the one, true God. That is what we are called to do when we come to the altar at Mass. The heart of our Faith is worship, and so it is devastating when we don't know how to worship—when we show up and just watch rather than participate in adoring our loving God.

If we're going to understand how to worship—if we're going to come to the altar—we need to know what the heart of worship is. The heart of worship is not singing a song. It is not saying a prayer. No, the heart of worship is *sacrifice*. At the center of nearly every religion throughout the history of the world is worship, and this worship is nearly always marked by sacrifice. And where are sacrifices offered? On an altar.

The altar is the place of sacrifice, where we offer the gift to God. The altar is the place where we worship.

This is why the Temple was so important to the Jewish people. It was the only place where sacrifices could be offered. There were synagogues, which were places of prayer and learning. But the only place they could truly *worship*—that is, offer sacrifice on the altar—was in the Temple.

> Where your altar is reveals where your heart is—because worship reveals *whose* you are.

So the Jewish people would go to the synagogue in their town to pray on every Sabbath, to learn about God, and to have community. But to worship, they needed to go to the Temple in Jerusalem because only the Temple had the altar of sacrifice. After the Temple was destroyed and the Jews were sent into exile in Babylon, one of their prayers of lament was, in effect, "What do we do now? How can we possibly worship the Lord?" Since there was no longer a Temple, there was no altar—so no sacrifice, no proper worship of God.

Gathering around that altar and performing that sacrifice gave the Jewish people their identity as God's people. It reminded them of who they were, and it reminded them of *whose* they were. Something very similar is true for us: where your altar is reveals where your heart is—because worship reveals *whose* you are.

FREE OF RIVALS

Before God could lead the people of Israel into worship, he had to defeat their old rivals—the idols. During the Exodus, the ten plagues God brought on Egypt were not arbitrary. They were showing the Lord, the true God, defeating the false gods of Egypt—the rivals to his proper place in the hearts of his people.

This is why the Lord commanded the Israelites to celebrate the Passover meal by slaughtering, roasting, and eating an unblemished lamb and then marking their doorposts and lintels with its blood. In Egypt, lambs were sacred. The people of Israel, then, needed to kill this final rival before God could reveal to them true worship—to show that there would be no going back. They would then be able to gather at the altar of the Lord and offer up true sacrifice.

In Exodus 24, we read how Moses told the people the laws and commands of the Lord, and then he built an altar at the foot of Mount Sinai. The people told Moses that they would do all that the Lord had commanded. Then Moses slaughtered young bulls, sprinkling half of their blood on the altar and half on the people. The people ate and drank in the presence of God.

At Mass, we hear the Word of God proclaimed in the Scriptures and hear it explained in the homily, then offer the sacrifice. We eat and drink in the presence of God. We are set free from all "rivals" so we can worship God in true and eternal worship. We get to come to the altar.

GIVING, NOT GETTING

This is an amazing gift. Yet often when we go to Mass, we do it because we have to. We just don't feel like going. In fact, a lot of times people will say that they don't "get anything out of Mass." Maybe you feel like that, too. But let's go back to the purpose of the altar.

Jews throughout Israel would travel with families to Jerusalem for Passover. They would bring a lamb with them (or would acquire a lamb there). The lamb had to be a year-old male and unblemished. They would carry that lamb around their shoulders so that it did not get hurt. Since it would live with them for a week, they would begin to love the lamb, so sacrificing this lamb cost them something because it had value in their hearts.

THE LAMB WITHOUT BLEMISH

"Tell all the congregation of Israel that on the tenth day of this month they shall take every man a lamb according to their fathers' houses, a lamb for a household ... Your lamb shall be without blemish, a male a year old; you shall take it from the sheep or from the goats; and you shall keep it until the fourteenth day of this month" (Exodus 12:3, 5–6).

They would bring this innocent and beautiful creature that mattered to them to the Temple, to the outside wall where a priest would hand them a knife to slit the lamb's throat. The priest would hold bowls to catch the blood as it drained from the throat of the lamb. A line of priests passed the bowl from priest to priest, all the way into the Temple, to the altar. This was not actually a sacrifice until the final priest poured the blood of the lamb onto the altar. Then the people would skin the lamb, bring it home, and eat it that night.

As we have said, the place of sacrifice is the altar. The altar is where we have the opportunity to actually *worship*—and not just watch. The problem is, we have been conditioned just to watch, to seek to be entertained. So it is no surprise that we begin to base the value of worship on what we get out of it.

For the Jewish people, offering a sacrifice to God at the altar is what was important. It was not about them. When we say we don't get anything out of Mass, this means that we have made Mass about *us*. But the heart of worship is sacrifice, not whether we "get something" from it or whether we are entertained.

Once I was traveling with a husband and wife to the airport. On our way, we stopped briefly to visit a well-known megachurch that the woman had attended before she was married. The husband was Catholic, and they had agreed at the time to attend a Mass at his church and then a service at her church. The wife thought she would "win" with the dynamic service at her church. While her husband appreciated the excitement of the music and the preaching, he asked, "But when do you *worship*? When do you stop and let it be about God?"

As we have seen, the heart of religion is worship—and the heart of worship is sacrifice. The place of sacrifice is an altar. It doesn't matter how we feel in our worship. It matters *where our altar is*. Do we offer sacrifice to the Lord, or do we have an altar in our hearts to ourselves?

We need to come to the altar of the Lord. We need to worship, not just watch. This is the call to love the Lord our God with everything we have and everything we are.

REFLECT

What is your primary motivation for going to Mass on Sunday? Take a moment to be introspective and honest in your answer.

The heart of worship is sacrifice. What are the most sacrificial moments of Mass—when we offer something and then receive something? Discuss why it may be easy to miss these moments.

Should we see the altar at church as a place of sacrifice or as a "dining table"? Discuss how our view of the altar affects how we approach the Mass.

Share one thing you believe might help you show up prepared to truly worship the next time you go to Mass.

PRAY

The people of Israel had one place to offer their sacrifice—the Temple—yet we can come into the presence of the Father at any moment of our lives. They had the Spirit of God near to them when he spoke through the prophets, yet we are blessed to have this *same* Spirit within us through grace. They were required to offer their gift of sacrifice at the Temple once a year, yet we are blessed beyond comprehension by Jesus' gift of himself in the Holy Eucharist.

With this in mind, make your prayer time today an altar of sacrifice to the Lord. Ask the Holy Spirit to call to mind those things in your life and in your heart that must be offered to him. There may be unhealthy things you are clinging to but no longer want in your life. Hand them over to your loving Father on the altar, trusting that he can take these things and use them for his glory.

You do not need to be afraid of the altar. Know that it is not a place of destruction but of transformation! If bread and wine offered on the altar can become the Body, Blood, Soul, and Divinity of our Lord Jesus Christ, then think of the amazing things he can do with your life when it is offered to him.

ACT ///

This Sunday, arrive for Mass a few minutes earlier than usual and spend that time reflecting on the call to come to the altar to worship God.

CHAPTER 2

LEARNING TO WORSHIP

In the 1990s, the singer Bonnie Raitt had a hit song entitled "I Can't Make You Love Me." The lyrics from that song continue to stick with me. She laments that it is impossible to *make* someone care about you.

Those lyrics ring especially true for me when I think about the Mass. While the cry of my heart is for worship to matter to everyone, I cannot *make* you care about it. I cannot make it important to you. The truth is, if you don't care—and just go to Mass to "check off the box" because you are Catholic—then I cannot make you care.

There is no higher thing we can do as human beings than to worship God in the way he has asked us to worship him.

To be honest, though, that kills me. Because, as we have said, the heart of religion, of everything we do, is worship. And the heart of worship is sacrifice. There is truly no greater human act we can do than worship God. Yes, there are many good things we can do. If we have the opportunity to save a busload of kids, that's obviously good. But there is no higher thing we can do as human beings than to worship God in the way he has asked us to worship him.

The reality is, though, even if we know and believe that the heart of religion is worship and the heart of worship is sacrifice, the Mass might still be a mystery. We might genuflect and cross ourselves, kneel and stand at the right times, say the right words—but still not really know what it all means. Shouldn't worshipping God be simpler and more natural?

A friend of mine and his wife were raised as evangelical Christians. At one point, they attended Mass for the first time and were inspired. They both eventually became Catholic. But my friend's wife lamented that the Mass seems complex and even confusing. As an evangelical Christian, her experience of worship had been more natural, flowing out of the heart; it was simple and easy to understand. Maybe you agree with the idea that Mass should be easy to understand and should just "come from the heart" if it is true worship.

Then my friend reminded his wife that, before becoming Catholic, they had spent their whole lives studying the Bible. We believe that the Bible is God's Word, but it certainly is not always simple and easy to understand. This is why we have Bible studies. So if the Bible is not always clear, then why do we think that the worship of God should always be easy to understand? If we need to learn about the meaning of the Bible, shouldn't we also need to learn about the meaning of the Mass?

So let's take a look at the most amazing aspects of worship.

THE WHAT AND THE WHO

First, let's take a look at the *what*. What exactly are we doing at Mass? To put it simply, we are offering up the sacrifice of Jesus the Son to the Father through the power of the Holy Spirit. In the letter to the Hebrews, we read that Jesus offered himself up once for all (Hebrews 7:27; 9:25). So we are not *re-sacrificing* Our Lord in the Mass; we are *re-presenting* his sacrifice on the Cross on the altar, in the form of the Eucharist.

ONE SACRIFICE

"He has no need, like those high priests, to offer sacrifices daily, first for his own sins and then for those of the people; he did this once for all when he offered up himself" (Hebrews 7:27).

Now *who* are we offering? The Son. Some say that we are merely offering bread and wine as symbols of Jesus, not really Jesus. But let's see what Scripture has to say on this question. At the Last Supper, Jesus took bread, saying, "This is my body which is given for you" (Luke 22:19). He then took the cup of wine and said, "This chalice which is poured out for you is the new covenant in my blood" (Luke 22:20). So we are offering Jesus in the Holy Sacrifice of the Mass.

Some say that he didn't really mean it like that. Again, what does the Bible say? In chapter 6 of John's Gospel, Jesus miraculously feeds five thousand people with five loaves and two fish. The next day, the people come looking for him, not because they believe in him as the Messiah but because they want more food.

Jesus, of course, knows why they are looking for him. So he tells them that he has food for them and, if they eat it, they will live forever. He starts by saying, "I am the bread of life; he who comes to me shall not hunger, and he who believes in me shall never thirst" (John 6:35). Many present become uneasy at these words. But Jesus doubles down. In John 6:51, he says, "I am the living bread which came down from heaven; if any one eats of this bread, he will live for ever; and the bread which I shall give for the life of the world is my flesh."

Now if those who were there and heard these shocking words knew Jesus was just speaking figuratively or symbolically, there would be no issue. After all, he had said he was the Good Shepherd, while everyone knew he was a carpenter. He had also said that he was the vine, and they knew he wasn't a plant. Throughout his public ministry, Jesus used many metaphors to describe himself and the Kingdom of God. Here, though, the Gospel of John reports that the Jews quarreled among themselves, saying, "How can this man give us his flesh to eat?" (John 6:52). Why would they ask this if they were not taking his words literally?

If Jesus was speaking symbolically, he had every opportunity to correct them. Yet he says not once, not twice, but five times, in a solemn oath, "Truly, truly, I say to you, unless you eat the flesh of the Son of man and drink his blood, you have no life in you" (John 6:53).

And he doesn't stop there, saying, "He who eats my flesh and drinks my blood has eternal life, and I will raise him on the last day. For my flesh is food indeed, and my blood is drink indeed. He who eats my flesh and drinks my blood abides in me and I in him. As the living Father sent me, and I live because of the Father, so he who eats me will live because of me" (John 6:54–57).

It is clear that those present took Jesus at his word, based on the reaction of some. As we read, "Many of his disciples, when they heard it, said, 'This is a hard saying; who can listen to it?'… After this many of his disciples drew back and no longer walked with him" (John 6:60, 66). This is the only time in the Gospels when people stopped following Jesus due to one of his teachings. And it was over his teaching that he is truly present in the Eucharist. The Eucharist is not just a symbol of Jesus. It actually *is* Jesus.

When I was about sixteen, I had a conversion experience. I was in my parents' house reading a book that spoke about the real presence of Jesus in the Eucharist. I had gone to Catholic school and Mass every Sunday, but this had gone over my head. I remember running downstairs to my siblings and telling them, "Did you know that the Eucharist is really Jesus?" I was blown away. It changed everything. I used to hate going to Mass, but that day changed everything because I realized God didn't just want me to come and sing a song. He didn't just want me to come and listen to a priest go on and on. He wanted me to come to the altar because *he* is there.

For the first 1,500 years of Christianity, all Christians—both Catholics and Orthodox— understood Jesus' words in John 6 literally. That's right. One hundred percent of Christians believed that Jesus is truly present in the Eucharist.[2]

> For the first 1,500 years of Christianity, *all* Christians believed that Jesus is truly present in the Eucharist.

If this is not true, then Catholics for two thousand years have been the worst idolaters who have ever existed. Why? Because we *worship* Jesus in the Eucharist. We go on our knees before Jesus in the Eucharist and say, "That's you." In the book of Exodus, some of the Israelites worshipped the golden calf for a single day—and the Lord quickly destroyed them for their idolatry. The Mass has been offered every day, at every moment throughout the world, for two thousand years. Do you think that same God would allow his Church to be defined by idolatry for two millennia?

THE WHY

So what are we doing at Mass? We are offering up the sacrifice of the Son to the Father. Who are we offering? Jesus the Son. After I realized that Jesus is really present in the Eucharist, every time I went to Mass, I went to see the miracle. If you've known this already, maybe that's why you come to Mass, too. I'm Catholic and not anything else because I come to hear the priest say, "This is my body" and "This is my blood." I come to see the miracle.

But the point of the Mass is not "just" that Jesus transforms bread and wine into his Body and Blood. This is setting the stage for something even greater. We are not present merely to witness the Eucharist as a *noun* but to participate in it as a *verb*. Jesus changes what was bread and wine into his own Body and Blood so we too can offer the sacrifice, not just watch this miracle.

After the Preparation of the Gifts, the priest asks us to pray that his sacrifice and ours will be acceptable to God. Why do we offer up the sacrifice of the Son to the Father at every Mass? For the praise and glory of the Father's name—and for our good and the good of all the Church. Every time we lift up the sacrifice of the Son to the Father, what happens? The Father is glorified and the world is redeemed—not because we are "re-sacrificing" Jesus but because we are re-presenting that one sacrifice, once for all, to the Father. And we get to be a part of it.

ONE SACRIFICE

In chapter 10 of the letter to the Hebrews, we read that Jesus doesn't have to offer sacrifice again and again. He offered it once for all when he offered his very self. He did this in two places, in two ways, one time: on the Cross on Calvary, and at the Last Supper: "And he took bread, and when he had given thanks he broke it and gave it to them, saying, 'This is my body which is given for you. Do this in remembrance of me.' And likewise the chalice after supper, saying, 'This chalice which is poured out for you is the new covenant in my blood'" (Luke 22:19–20).

We know what the people of Israel did to worship at Passover. Each family would take an unblemished lamb that was precious to them and bring it to the Temple. They would present the lamb to the priests as a sacrifice to the Lord, and the priests would collect its blood and pour it onto the altar. The family would then take the lamb home and consume it.

At the Temple, the sacrifice of the lamb was completed when the blood was poured out on the altar. At the Last Supper, Jesus is saying, "This is my blood poured out." And then he commands his disciples, "Do this in memory of me." In these powerful words, Jesus makes it absolutely clear how he wants us to worship him. *Offer up the sacrifice.* Offer up *me*, once for all, blood poured out, body given over.

At Mass, we take what is precious to us and present it to the Father. When the priest, during the Consecration, says, "This is my body given for you," he elevates the host to show us the sacrifice. This is the Lamb—Jesus—being sacrificed. Then he holds up the chalice, saying it is the blood of the lamb being sacrificed.

Then, we pray for God's glory and for the salvation of the world in the Great Amen. The priest takes the Lamb, Jesus himself, and lifts him up to the Father, saying, "Through him, with him, and in him, in the unity of the Holy Spirit, all glory and honor is yours, Almighty Father, forever and ever." The Great Amen is supposed to sound out. In the early Church, Christians would cry out so powerfully that the walls in the church would shake!

After the Great Amen, we come forward to consume the Lamb. Every time we show up and do this—even if we are distracted or sick or have a bunch of kids crawling all over us—the Father is glorified. Every time we do this, the world is redeemed. From this moment until the moment we step into heaven, the Father will be glorified. Because we are not just present at Mass to *watch* but to *worship*.

BEHOLD THE LOVE OF GOD

In the Temple in Jerusalem, the Ark of the Covenant was present in its innermost room, the Holy of Holies. Immediately before the Holy of Holies was the Holy Place, in which there were three sacred objects: the altar of incense, the golden lampstand (or menorah) with candles burning, and a table with twelve loaves of bread—the Bread of the Presence. The Hebrew word translated here as "presence" can also mean "face," so this is the bread of the very face of God.

During the high holy days, the priest would go into the Holy Place and come out with the Bread of the Presence. He would hold it aloft over the people and say: "Behold the love of God for you." And they would look up and see the Bread of the Presence. They would behold the love of the Lord for them. The Eucharist is the fulfillment of the Bread of the Presence because it truly *is* Jesus, God Incarnate. As he elevates the Eucharist at Mass, the priest says, "Behold the Lamb of God." Behold the love of God for us.

As we are praying after receiving Holy Communion, we should reflect on the amazing reality that we have consumed the very love of God in the Eucharist. During Mass, we behold the love of God for us—and then receive this love in the Body, Blood, Soul, and Divinity of his Son.

REFLECT

What is one thing in your life that you know very well and care about?

Share or journal about any frustrations or confusion you have felt about attending Mass.

Have you ever had a profound awareness of Jesus' presence in the Eucharist? Please share and discuss.

How can an understanding that Jesus' offering of himself is re-presented in the Mass change how you worship at Mass? Discuss.

Every time we offer the once-for-all sacrifice of the Son to the Father in the Mass, the world is redeemed and the Father is glorified. How could you participate more intentionally at Mass so that the Father is glorified even more fully in you and salvation is extended through you?

PRAY

For many reasons, worship does not come naturally to most of us. We can be confused as to the *who*, *what*, *why*, and *how* of worship. We need to *learn* to worship. As you begin your time of prayer today, use it as a time of preparation for the next time you go to Mass.

First, ask the Holy Spirit to prepare your heart and mind for worship. Remember that you are not going to Mass simply to watch and be entertained by great preaching or inspiring music. You are going to a specific church at a specific time to offer the one true and eternal sacrifice to God! In other words, you are going to Mass to *make an offering* to him.

Next, ask the Spirit to prepare your heart for the *type* of sacrifice you will make. We can be tempted to make our worship be about the fact that we are offering ourselves to God. Though it is good and necessary to offer our whole being to him, we actually go to Mass to offer *the Son to the Father*!

Lastly, remember *why* you are making this sacrifice—for the glory of God. You are participating in the "re-presenting" of the sacrifice of the Son to the Father to bring glory to him! The whole goal of our prayer life—and the primary goal of the Mass—is to worship God, to be sanctified by his glory. Seek to carry these meditations into Mass with you!

ACT ///

This week at Mass, stay for a few minutes at the end and thank God that you have just beheld and consumed his love in the Holy Eucharist.

CHAPTER 3

KINGDOM PRIESTHOOD

Google knows me. Knowing that I would be entertained by a website full of strange exercise devices from the not-too-distant past, it directed me to such a site automatically. Apparently, there were devices that sent an electromagnetic shock through your body to make you fit and healthy. This reminded me that my grandmother had a metal platform you would stand on, with a canvas belt that you would put around your waist. The belt would then vibrate to "shake the fat off," increase your circulation, and make you healthy in the process. Of course, none of these gadgets work. So they ended up being nothing more than a waste of time and money.

Maybe you have been to the gym and seen a guy on a recumbent bike—you know, the ones you lie back on and pedal—reading or watching TV, letting the pedals move his feet for him. This person really thinks that he is working out. But unless he is in a "cool down" (or is unable to physically exercise more than this), he is wasting his time.

We do this with things other than exercise. Students sometimes say they studied for the entire weekend in the library or a coffee shop. But often if they added up the amount of time they actually spent studying, it would be minimal. Instead, they watched other people, spent time on social media, and talked to friends. Like the hours spent in the gym not working out, it's a waste of time.

I recently came across a documentary about Sister Clare, who grew up in Ireland in a tough family and a rough neighborhood. As a young adult, she rejected Christianity, but when Jesus finally won over her heart, and she became convinced that he loved her, she discerned a call to become a religious sister—a bride of Christ.

She was sent to work in Ecuador, where she died in an earthquake at age 32. She once had said that her only fear was that she would die without having given all of herself. Her fear was that she would look back and realize that she had wasted the opportunity to love Christ completely. This blew my heart open.

SISTER CLARE MARIA OF THE TRINITY AND THE HEART OF MARY
1982–2016

Born Clare Theresa Crockett, Sister Clare died while serving in Ecuador during the 2016 earthquake there. Her intercession has reportedly led to several miraculous healings, leading to calls to open her cause for canonization as a saint.

CALLED TO LOVE

We began this booklet by talking about our call to love God. As we said before, the Church has defined love as willing the good of the other. And so, when spouses love each other, their love is not just romantic feelings or feelings of affection—it is choosing to do something. It's choosing to will the good of that person. That is very important. Whether I love a stranger or whether I love my mom—that's how we love.

When it comes to God, we're made to love God above everything, above everyone. But here is the question we asked earlier: If love is willing the good of the other, how do we love God?

We talked about the answer. We can love God in three ways. We love God by loving others, by obeying him, and by worshipping him.

We love God when we obey him by worshipping him as he has asked us to worship him. Why is this the way we love God? Because the heart of religion is worship. We talked about this.

When we come to the altar to worship, what do we give to God? The heart of worship is not feelings. The heart of worship is always going to be sacrifice. Sacrifice is the heart of worship, which is the heart of religion, which is the heart of what it is to love God.

A little while ago, I had an interview with a Catholic journalist, and he asked a question. He said, "Have you noticed that, because of COVID, fewer people are returning to in-person Mass?" And I talked about how important it is that everyone gets back to Mass. If they can be at Mass at all, then they need to be at Mass, absolutely. And he said, "That's right, you can't just watch Mass online because the point is to receive the Eucharist." And I had to stop and say, "Actually, no, that's not true." One of the gifts of the Mass is that we get to receive the Eucharist. That is an awesome gift. Jesus made it very, very clear that unless we eat the flesh of the Son of Man and drink his blood, we do not have life. So, yes, it is very, very important to be able to receive the Eucharist.

But the point of the Mass is not to receive Holy Communion. The point of Mass is to offer the sacrifice of the Son of God to the Father. The point of the Mass is to offer to the Father the sacrifice of the Last Supper and the sacrifice of Calvary, which are brought into one at every Mass.

The whole point is to love God. Sacrifice is the heart of loving God, and so the point of our lives is to worship God in the Mass by offering the greatest sacrifice any of us could ever possibly hope or even imagine we can be part of.

THE MINISTERIAL PRIESTHOOD

Yet how often do we, as Catholics, show up at Mass but we do not do it in a way that makes a difference? Do we go and just watch? Or do we show up and truly worship? Do we show up ready to truly present Jesus who is really present in the Eucharist to the Father in the power of the Holy Spirit? This question is at the heart of how we *come to the altar*.

There is so much more about coming to the altar to worship than just watching—and it has everything to do with the priesthood. Without the priesthood, we have no Mass and no Eucharist—no sacrifice, and therefore no true worship.

We see in the Bible that Jesus chose twelve men, the Apostles, to participate in his priesthood in a unique way. We see this throughout the Gospels. At the end of Matthew, Jesus tells his disciples, "Go therefore and make disciples of all nations, baptizing them in the name of the Father and of the Son and of the Holy Spirit" (Matthew 28:19). Then, in John, he says that those whose sins the Apostles forgive are forgiven, and those whose sins they do not forgive are not forgiven (see John 20:23); in other words, they have the authority from Jesus to forgive sins in his name. We see him sending them out to heal the sick; they are commissioned to act sacramentally, with his power.

At the Last Supper, Jesus makes his Apostles his first priests when he says, "Take this all of you, and eat. This is my Body. Take this all of you and drink, this is my Blood. Do this in memory of me." In effect, Jesus "ordains" them and gives them the ability to consecrate the Eucharist—to make him truly present, Body, Blood, Soul, and Divinity, in what looks like bread and wine. He gives them a participation in his one priesthood. As a ministerial priest, I share in the one priesthood of Christ because of my ordination.

> Because of their ordination, priests share in the one priesthood of Christ.

Jesus called both Peter and Judas as Apostles. Around the year 400, St. Augustine said that when Peter baptizes, it is Christ who baptizes, and when Judas baptizes, it is Christ who baptizes.[3] Why? Because whether a priest is a saint or a notorious sinner, it is Jesus who acts through him when he celebrates the sacraments.

From the beginning, the Apostles saw themselves as being responsible for passing on their ministerial priesthood through their successors, the bishops. In the Acts of the Apostles, we read that they consecrated Paul and Barnabas through the laying on of hands (see Acts 13). These bishops then ordained others, and so on, down to the present day. The bishops also ordained men as priests to assist them in their ministry.

Why are priests consecrated to baptize, forgive sins, and celebrate the Eucharist? So that they can bring us into contact with God in a way that is transformative, in a way that makes us holy. Then, we can bring this sanctity into our families and friendships and workplaces, wherever we go and to everyone we meet.

THE PRIESTHOOD OF THE KINGDOM

While there are thousands of ministerial priests on earth, the first chapter of the book of Revelation in the Bible tells us that Jesus has established a kingdom of priests—all those who are baptized share in his priesthood.

At our baptism, the priest (or deacon) anointed us with oil to give us a share in Christ's ministry as priest, prophet, and king. So if we have been baptized, we have been consecrated and anointed, set apart to be priests of the kingdom.

As the Church teaches, every baptized Christian participates in the "common priesthood of all the faithful"—that is, the priesthood of the kingdom—with some men also being ordained to the ministerial priesthood (see the *Catechism of the Catholic Church* 1547). As priests of the kingdom, all of us are called to forgive those who have hurt us. But those who are ministerial priests can actually forgive sins in Jesus' name, anoint the sick, confect the Eucharist, and offer up the sacrifice of Jesus to the Father through the power of the Holy Spirit. So there is one priesthood of Christ, but two different "participations" in this one priesthood.

FROM THE *CATECHISM*

"The ministerial or hierarchical priesthood of bishops and priests, and the common priesthood of all the faithful participate, 'each in its own proper way, in the one priesthood of Christ.' While being 'ordered one to another,' they differ essentially. In what sense? While the common priesthood of the faithful is exercised by the unfolding of baptismal grace—a life of faith, hope, and charity, a life according to the Spirit— the ministerial priesthood is at the service of the common priesthood" (CCC 1547).

Here is the problem, though. Often, we just show up at Mass and watch as a ministerial priest offers up the sacrifice. But the Lord Jesus did not from all eternity call people to be his sons and daughters only to come to Mass and *watch* the priest worship.

When we just *show up* at Mass, we "waste" our priesthood—and the Father is not glorified as he should be. We forget or we never knew that what we're supposed to be doing here is worshipping. We're supposed to be offering the sacrifice. We're supposed to be uniting our hearts to the sacrifice of Jesus.

When the priest is praying those words, we should not just be waiting for him to finish. My part as the ministerial priest is to pray the prayers. Our part together is to be saying, "Lord, receive this sacrifice. May you be glorified. May this world be sanctified. May this world be changed and transformed." But if we just show up and sit and watch, of course we're unchanged.

We are not here to watch or be entertained. We're here to offer up the sacrifice of the Son to the Father in the power of the Holy Spirit.

LIVING SACRIFICES

So how do we *not* waste our priesthood?

Shortly after I was ordained, I read a phenomenal book by Archbishop Fulton Sheen called *The Priest Is Not His Own*. It's definitely worth reading, for anyone. At one point, Archbishop Sheen writes that priests may sometimes forget that Jesus not only *offers* the sacrifice, he *is* the sacrifice; he is both the priest and victim. Archbishop Sheen says that while priests should be excited to celebrate Mass—that is, to offer the sacrifice—they need to be just as eager to be the victim.[4]

What I invite you to do as priests of the kingdom is what Archbishop Sheen invites ministerial priests to do: not only to go to Mass and offer the sacrifice but to go to Mass and *be* the sacrifice. That is why St. Paul tells us to offer our bodies as a living sacrifice (see Romans 12:1). The third Eucharistic Prayer asks that the Father make us an "eternal offering."

And the fourth Eucharistic Prayer asks that we might become a "living sacrifice" in Christ for the glory of God.

In Baptism, each of us became a child of God—and a temple of the Holy Spirit. A temple is the place where the deity abides, so being a temple of the Holy Spirit means the Holy Spirit dwells inside each of us. In the ancient world, temples were places of sacrifice. Because we have been made into temples of the Holy Spirit, we are called both to offer sacrifice and to be the sacrifice.

My prayer is that no Catholics will ever show up to Mass and just watch but instead they will come and worship. My prayer is that they will never just show up to Mass and waste their kingdom priesthood but they will intentionally offer the sacrifice of the Son to the Father with the ministerial priest. My prayer is that, from now on, all will *be* the sacrifice along with Jesus—each time they come to the altar.

REFLECT

Is there an area of your life in which you do not give all of yourself? What about when it comes to the Mass?

The ministerial priesthood is essential to the life of the Church, since without priests there is no Eucharist, no sacrifice, and no worship. Think of a priest who has been a blessing in your life. What qualities does he have? What about his ministry has blessed you?

How does the common priesthood of the faithful—the kingdom priesthood—bring God's grace to the world? Offer some practical examples.

As a kingdom priest, you are called to *be* a sacrifice. Have you ever thought of yourself in this way—as one called to offer your life as a sacrifice for God? How can this understanding change how you approach prayer and how you enter into the Mass?

PRAY

The idea that you are a "priest of the kingdom" by virtue of your baptism might be new to you. Maybe you have been Catholic your whole life but have never considered this. Or perhaps you did not grow up going to Mass and you are encountering the supernatural depths of worshipping Jesus for the first time.

Regardless of where you are coming from, as you enter into prayer today, ask the Holy Spirit to show you how you can embrace your role as a "priest of the kingdom." Pray for a deeper awareness of how you are called to unite yourself to the sacrifice in the Mass. Pray that your prayer at Mass can begin to come from the depths of your heart. Allow the Holy Spirit the time to speak to your heart as you meditate on the truth of your kingdom priesthood.

Lastly, ask the Lord to show you how you may have been wasting your kingdom priesthood until now. Ask him to show you how you can be a better priest of the kingdom in your daily life. Every day is filled with opportunities to live out your relationship with God in the priestly way to which he has called you!

ACT ///

In your prayer this week, give thanks to God for the gift of the priesthood. Ask God to bless and strengthen the priests you know.

CHAPTER 4

HALLOWED, NOT HOLLOW

A number of years ago, I knew a missionary who proposed to another missionary. It was a wonderful and joyous occasion, and he got her an incredible ring. After talking with the guy, though—and doing some research—I discovered that the diamond ring industry is really just a racket.

Until the early nineteenth century, diamonds truly were a rare commodity, found only in a few dry riverbeds in India. In 1867, though, massive diamond fields were discovered in South Africa. Tons of diamonds then flooded the market, and they were no longer rare or precious—or valuable.

So the De Beers Consolidated Diamond Corporation ingeniously cornered the entire world diamond supply. Despite their best efforts, though, they were unable to sell many diamonds. In fact, in the 1930s, the average diamond engagement ring cost only eighty dollars. To address this, the De Beers company hired a New York marketing firm to develop one of the most successful campaigns in history. This marketing campaign literally *created* demand by portraying diamond engagement rings as something every couple just had to have.

How did the company accomplish this? By going to high schools and telling the senior boys that a good diamond engagement ring would really show their love for their future wife. They told the senior girls that if a guy really loved her, he would give her a diamond engagement ring worth three months' salary. In addition, the diamond marketers highlighted celebrities, royalty, and other important people wearing diamonds.[5]

The reality, of course, is that a diamond itself is worthless. There are so many that it really is just another rock. And yet, even though the diamond itself is not valuable, a diamond ring is valuable because of what it shows. Diamonds have become the symbol of true love—of forever devotion.

As a priest, I will never be engaged, of course. However, if I were not a priest and I got engaged, I too would get the best ring I could afford even though I know it is a racket. Why? Because I would want to show my love for my future bride.

An expensive diamond ring is a sign of love. It represents the sacrifice someone is willing to make for the person he loves. What could have been an empty gesture, a hollow offering, ends up not being empty at all. Why? Because of love. Love fills up that offering and transforms it.

CHANGED

We can think about the Magi, the three wise men who came to worship the baby Jesus. We celebrate their coming on the feast of the Epiphany, a few days after Christmas. They were some of the first people who ever worshipped Jesus Christ incarnate on this earth. They journeyed from afar, and they brought Jesus gifts of gold, frankincense, and myrrh. They offered him those gifts. It was a sacrifice, and it was not empty.

The gifts that the Magi offered to Jesus all mean something. Theologians have said that the gold is a sign of Jesus as king, that the frankincense is a sign of Jesus as a priest who offers incense, and the myrrh is a sign of Jesus' death and his being anointed at death. The gifts that the Magi offered symbolized that Jesus was ultimately going to be not just the priest who offers the sacrifice but also the victim being offered in the sacrifice.[6]

These Magi came before the Lord God incarnate with these three gifts. They worshipped him, they bowed down before him, and they offered him their best.

THE MAGI

"Now when Jesus was born in Bethlehem of Judea in the days of Herod the king, behold Wise Men from the East came to Jerusalem, saying, 'Where is he who has been born king of the Jews? For we have seen his star in the East, and have come to worship him' ... and behold, the star which they had seen in the East went before them, till it came to rest over the place where the child was ... and going into the house they saw the child with Mary his mother, and they fell down and worshiped him. Then, opening their treasures, they offered him gifts, gold and frankincense and myrrh. And being warned in a dream not to return to Herod, they departed to their own country by another way" (Matthew 2:1–2, 9, 11–12).

Scripture says that after the Magi offered their gifts of gold, frankincense, and myrrh, they departed for their home by another way. The saints would say, "Yes, that is what is supposed to happen. I came to the Lord one way, but when I worshipped him, it changed me, and I had to go home a different way. I couldn't go home the same way. I couldn't return the same person I was when I walked into the Lord's presence."

But the question is, does worship make a difference in my life? I think a lot of times we show up to Mass and leave unchanged. The Mass is supposed to make all the difference in the world, but it does not make a difference in our lives.

FIRSTFRUITS

As we have seen, we are called to come to the altar and worship by offering the sacrifice of Jesus himself at Mass. The Mass re-presents the sacrifice of Jesus out of love to the Father. It is not just valuable; it is infinitely valuable.

Yet how many times do we go to Mass and feel empty? We know that the Mass is the worship that Jesus himself gave us, his own sacrifice, so it cannot be empty or hollow. The problem is not the Mass. So let's look at why we might walk away unchanged.

It might be that we just didn't expect that anything would happen; we didn't expect anything should change. We went to Mass to check the box and now we're leaving. But how could we possibly come into contact with the true, living God and not be changed? The whole point of the Mass is loving the Lord in such a way that we are not the same anymore. So how can we remain the same? I think part of it is because we're missing two things.

> If I go to Mass and return unchanged, it's probably because I didn't offer anything.

First, we are missing out on the reality that we are here to sacrifice. We are here to unite our prayers with the prayers of the ministerial priest at the altar, who is united to the great High Priest, Jesus.

There is also a second reason why we might be unchanged by the Mass. The Magi offered Jesus gold for a king, frankincense for a priest, and myrrh for the one who died. Their gifts symbolized that Jesus is not just the priest who offers the sacrifice, he is the sacrifice that is offered—and so are you.

If I go to Mass and return unchanged, it's probably because I didn't offer anything. I'll say that again. If I go to Mass and I leave the same way I walked in, it's because I didn't offer anything. I did not give God anything. I didn't give him what I was afraid of. I didn't give him what I love. I didn't give him access to my hopes. I didn't give him access to my weaknesses. I just showed up and watched.

This is hinted at in the letter to the Hebrews, where it says the high priest would enter into the Temple with blood that is not his own. The sacrifice did not cost him anything, so it could feel empty. In the Old Testament, this is why God asks his people to bring their "firstfruits" to him in worship (see Leviticus 23:10–14). So an Israelite farmer who raised wheat or grapes would give the first 10 percent of his crop to God, bringing it to the Temple as a sacrificial offering. A farmer who raised animals would bring the firstborn male of his flock to the Temple for sacrifice.

It was important for God's people to be willing to offer him their firstfruits to show the depth of trust and dependence on him. Of course, God does not need wheat or grapes or firstborn male animals. But he asks for his people to give him their firstfruits—their best—because *they* need it. We are no different than the people of Israel. If we don't give God our firstfruits—the best of what we have to offer—our worship is going to feel hollow and we will walk away unchanged.

Often, we give God our "leftovers." He gets our time when we don't have anything else to do. He gets the stuff we don't want anymore. We don't give him our best, only whatever is left. But what does that do to our relationship with him? What does it do to our hearts?

We need to give God our best, not just our leftovers.

Ladies, imagine that a guy invites you on a first date to a really nice restaurant and only orders one meal—for him. He eats until he is full, and then he says that you can have whatever is left, whatever he doesn't want. Well, it is probably a sure bet that you will not go out with him again. This is a recipe for a terrible relationship. But this is often how we live our lives when it comes to God.

For example, God calls us to pray. But how often do we pray only when we are done with everything else? God calls us to serve. But how often do we serve only when we don't have anything else to do? This is why God asks us to give him our firstfruits. When we plan our day, prayer should be the first thing on the agenda. When we plan our weekend, Mass needs to be the first thing we schedule our Sunday around. We need to give God our best, not just our leftovers.

INTENTIONAL, CONSEQUENTIAL, AND REPRESENTATIONAL

How do we know if we are really giving God our firstfruits? Here are three "markers" that show whether what we are offering is our best: *intentional*, *consequential*, and *representational*.

When what we are giving God is *intentional*, it is not an afterthought. It is not giving him whatever we have on hand. It is not pulling a random bill out of our pocket for the collection basket; it is having the check in the envelope before we go to Mass. It is planned ahead.

One way to do this is to make a decision to give the Lord everything. Then, whatever happens, we have planned ahead to offer it to him. On the morning of my ordination, I decided to go kayaking—mostly because I had seen a photo of St. John Paul II kayaking as a young priest. In doing so, I hurt my neck. It was the day of my ordination, a day I had been preparing for my whole life, and I was in a lot of pain. At one point during the Rite of Ordination, all the priests present embrace each of the newly ordained. Wow, did that hurt! But I had decided long before that one day that I would give the Lord everything. Regardless of how I felt, I made the intention to give him my firstfruits.

Giving our firstfruits also must be *consequential*—it needs to cost us something. It needs to be something that matters to us. In the ancient world, those who offered their firstborn male calf to the Lord truly were making a sacrifice. They were offering him their very livelihood. It *cost* them.

Firstfruits must also be *representational*. Sometimes, we offer God a time of prayer or work so we do not have to give him our hearts. It does not, then, represent any real sacrifice. In contrast, we can think of the example of the poor widow who gave the Lord all that she had, two copper coins, her entire livelihood (see Mark 12:41–44). They represented her desire for a relationship with the Lord.

THE WIDOW'S COINS

"And he sat down opposite the treasury, and watched the multitude putting money into the treasury. Many rich people put in large sums. And a poor widow came, and put in two copper coins, which make a penny. And he called his disciples to him, and said to them, 'Truly, I say to you, this poor widow has put in more than all those who are contributing to the treasury. For they all contributed out of their abundance; but she out of her poverty has put in everything she had, her whole living'" (Mark 12:41–44).

In Hebrews chapter 9, we read that Jesus has entered into the heavenly realms when he offered himself for us. Sometimes we might think that Jesus gave himself on the Cross in place of us. We might misunderstand this offering as meaning, "Father, I know your wrath and vengeance needs to be poured out on somebody, so instead of taking it out on these sinners, just take it out on me."

But God the Father did not need to take his vengeance out on anybody. In fact, as St. Thomas Aquinas tells us, it wasn't how much Jesus *suffered* on the Cross that saved us but how much he *loved* on the Cross.[7] The Crucifixion of Jesus was not about the Father pouring out his vengeance against sinners on his Son, but instead about the Son pouring out his love to the Father. When we come to Mass, we offer a representational sacrifice. We represent the love and sacrifice of Jesus back to the Father on behalf of ourselves and everyone we love.

HALLOWED, NOT HOLLOW

When we give the Lord our firstfruits, we end up truly worshipping during Mass rather than just watching Mass. We lay ourselves and those we love on the altar. Bringing our firstfruits—in a way that is intentional, consequential, and representational—is a tangible way of connecting with what Jesus has done and offered on the Cross.

So let's get back to diamond engagement rings—and wedding rings. If they are going to mean anything, they have to be given in an intentional, consequential, and representational way. They must truly be a *sign* of a couple's love and fidelity. They must truly *mean* something.

Following their wedding, the newly married couple must go out and proclaim, "This is a sign of my love. This represents my heart, which is yours. This is a sign of my fidelity, and I'm going to be faithful to you." It would be empty and hollow if a bride and groom said to each other, "Take this ring instead of my love, instead of my heart, instead of my fidelity," and then went off and lived their own life.

> Giving our firstfruits to the Lord both reveals and increases our trust in him.

The same is true when we offer our firstfruits at Mass. We don't say, "Take this instead of my heart, Lord." Instead, we say, "Take this as a sign of my heart, Lord. Now I am going to live the rest of my life like this." When we do this, our offering is made holy. It is hallowed, not hollow.

Giving our firstfruits to the Lord both reveals and increases our trust in him. This helps us to stop watching and start worshipping at Mass. When we do this, we make his sacrifice ours. We come to the altar.

REFLECT

What is the most meaningful gift you have received? What made it so valuable to you?

Have you felt "empty" or "hollow" at Mass? Discuss your experience.

When has God been calling you to offer your firstfruits to him? What is an area of your life in which you could be more consistent in giving them to the Lord?

Discuss ways you can make your offering of firstfruits to God more intentional, consequential, and representational.

PRAY

Seek to make your prayer today an altar of sacrifice to the Lord. Regardless of what your surroundings are at this moment, you *can* make it a time of holy worship. *Hallowed*, not hollow.

Begin by being intentional. You do not need to *feel* anything specific. Ask the Holy Spirit to show you where in your spiritual life you have been unintentional and unfocused—and to help you to intentionally place yourself in an attitude of prayer.

Then, ask the Lord to show you one thing in your life that you can offer him as worship. Remember that worship requires sacrifice, so pray about what you can offer to God that will come at a cost to you. Allow God to make your worship *consequential*.

Lastly, think about what you can offer to the Lord that would *represent your heart*, which is what you are truly offering him. For instance, you might turn your usual morning coffee time into dedicated prayer time. Through this, you can say, "Father, you know how much I love my morning quiet time. My heart is there. So I am giving this time to you because I love you." In this way, your act of sacrificial worship becomes a tangible representation of your heart for the Lord.

ACT ///

Reflect on how you can bring your firstfruits—as well as your heart and the people on your heart—to God in Mass this week.

CHAPTER 5

COME, HOLY SPIRIT

After Jesus rose from the dead, he gave a mission to the Apostles. The mission is not simple, but it is really straightforward. Jesus said, "As the Father has sent me, even so I send you" (John 20:21).

On the day of his Ascension, Jesus went on to give the Great Commission. He said, "Go therefore and make disciples of all nations, baptizing them in the name of the Father and of the Son and of the Holy Spirit, teaching them to observe all that I have commanded you; and behold, I am with you always, to the close of the age" (Matthew 28:19–20). The Great Commission is for all disciples, calling them to go everywhere throughout the world and to make disciples of all, baptizing them and teaching them.

In Acts 1:8, we hear more. Jesus told the disciples, "You shall receive power when the Holy Spirit has come upon you; and you shall be my witnesses in Jerusalem and in all Judea and Samaria and to the end of the earth" (Acts 1:8).

THE GREAT COMMISSION

"And Jesus came and said to them, 'All authority in heaven and on earth has been given to me. Go therefore and make disciples of all nations, baptizing them in the name of the Father and of the Son and of the Holy Spirit, teaching them to observe all that I have commanded you; and behold, I am with you always, to the close of the age'" (Matthew 28:18–20).

Jesus gave them a mission, and then he gave them the power to complete the mission.

This is how good God is. For every one of our lives, there is a call; for every one of our lives, there is some kind of mission. And for every Christian, the heart of the mission is exactly the Gospel, which is, "Go make disciples of all nations." But Jesus doesn't just give us the mission; he always gives us the power to complete the mission.

On their own, the disciples could not do anything. On our own, we could not do anything. Think about the mission Jesus gave when he said, "As the Father sent me, so I send you." Jesus was sent to bring salvation from sin. He healed the sick, bound up the wounded, set captives free, and brought mercy to the world. The Apostles were just people; they couldn't do that. But immediately, what did Jesus do? "When he had said this, he breathed on them, and said to them, 'Receive the Holy Spirit. If you forgive the sins of any, they are forgiven; if you retain the sins of any, they are retained'" (John 20:22–23).

Jesus did not just give them the call; he gave them the power to actually live out the call. He didn't just give them the mission; he gave them the strength, the gifts, and whatever it is that they needed to live the mission.

We have been talking about worship. We talked about the altar, the place of sacrifice, where we love God by worshipping him. We talked about what that sacrifice is—the one sacrifice of Jesus offered to the Father. We talked about our call as kingdom priests to unite ourselves to that sacrifice and offer our firstfruits in a way that is intentional, consequential, and representational. When we come to the altar at Mass, we are called to love the Lord in such a way that we are not the same anymore. So today we are going to talk about what happens when we walk out of Mass—when we walk away changed by the sacrifice that is offered on the altar.

THE POWER TO COMPLETE THE MISSION

On the day of the Ascension, Jesus gave the Great Commission to go and make disciples of all nations. Then, on the feast of Pentecost, God poured out the power to accomplish this mission. All of us share in this Great Commission to bring the Gospel of Jesus to the world.

If you say, "I can't do that on my own," you're right. But Jesus doesn't just give the call; he gives the power to live out the call. He does not just give the mission; he gives the strength and the gifts to accomplish the mission. He has given us the amazing gift of worshipping at the altar where we re-present his one sacrifice for the glory of the Father and the redemption of the world.

The Father has poured out the Holy Spirit upon the world. If you have been baptized, you received the Holy Spirit. If you have been confirmed, you received the Holy Spirit. The Father has filled you with the Holy Spirit. He has given you every gift that you need to accomplish the mission that he set apart for you. But we need to live out those gifts.

God has given us a call, and he has given us the strength to accomplish this call. Now he expects us to use it, just like he expected the Apostles to use the gifts he gave them. Jesus gave the Apostles the ability to forgive sins, so they went out and forgave sins. He gave them the power to offer the sacrifice of the Mass, so they went out and offered the sacrifice of the Mass. He gave them the ability to spread the Gospel, so they went out and spread the Gospel.

I don't want what Jesus has done in me to stop with me.

Think about how different it would have been if the Apostles had never gone out to spread the Gospel, forgive sins, and offer the Eucharist. On the feast of Pentecost, the people in Jerusalem were amazed because the Apostles preached and everyone could understand them in their own language. Imagine how different it would have been if the Holy Spirit had come down upon the Apostles with tongues of fire and they had just decided to take the gift and soak in it for their own enjoyment, as if it were a hot tub. That would be a waste of the gift. I think the Apostles were convinced they did not want to let what Jesus had done in them stop with them. That is the call for you and me, too. I don't want what Jesus has done in me to stop with me.

When I was in Confirmation class preparing to receive the Holy Spirit in the sacrament of Confirmation, I didn't know what to look forward to. People said, "Well, just pray for the gifts of the Holy Spirit." So, I prayed for wisdom, understanding, counsel, and knowledge, but I didn't know what those things really meant.

After I was confirmed, the *Catechism of the Catholic Church* came out, and one of the paragraphs in the *Catechism* talks about the five effects of Confirmation. And I thought, *That's what I would have liked to have known.* Some of the five effects are that Confirmation—which brings Pentecost to us now—establishes us more deeply as sons and daughters of God the Father. That's awesome. Confirmation binds us more closely to Jesus. That's awesome. Confirmation gives us an even greater abundance of those spiritual gifts that we received at our baptism. That's awesome. All of these gifts unite us even more closely to the Church.

God has made you his son or daughter. He has united himself in Jesus to you. He has made you part of the Church, giving you gifts of the Holy Spirit. Those are all things that God has done in you.

But the fifth effect of Confirmation is the one that I especially needed to know. The *Catechism* says that everyone who has been confirmed receives "a special strength of the Holy Spirit to spread and defend the faith by word and action ... to confess the name of Christ boldly, and never to be ashamed of the Cross" (CCC 1303).

The mission is, "Go make disciples." Jesus has given you the power to live out this. God has given you, in Confirmation, a special strength of the Holy Spirit to spread and defend the Faith by what you say and what you do, to proclaim the name of Jesus boldly, and never to be ashamed of the Cross and the sacrifice of the Cross, which is present at the altar.

THE SACRAMENT OF CONFIRMATION

"Confirmation brings an increase and deepening of baptismal grace:

- it roots us more deeply in the divine filiation which makes us cry, 'Abba! Father!';

- it unites us more firmly to Christ;

- it increases the gifts of the Holy Spirit in us;

- it renders our bond with the Church more perfect;

- it gives us a special strength of the Holy Spirit to spread and defend the faith by word and action as true witnesses of Christ, to confess the name of Christ boldly, and never to be ashamed of the Cross" (CCC 1303).

The question is not whether or not God has given us the gifts. The question is whether we are willing to use them. The question is not: "Has God called me? Is there a mission for me?" There is a mission. There is a call. The question is: "Am I willing to actually go out?"

WORTH SAVING

What is at stake is the salvation of the people of the world. The Great Commission is to go make disciples so that people can know God's love and can actually be his sons and daughters. That is what God wants. If we really believe that people are worth trying to save, we will not let what Jesus has done in us stop with us.

Years ago, I came across a man named Penn Jillette. He is an entertainer and has been an outspoken atheist. At one point, he made a video that struck me. After one of his shows, a man was waiting to talk to him. Penn Jillette said this man was really respectful. He came up to Penn and told him how much he liked the show. Then he handed him a small Bible. He must have known that Penn did not believe in God, but he said, "I wanted you to have this."

And Penn Jillette, reflecting on this, said, "If you believe that there's a heaven and hell and people could be going to hell … how much do you have to hate somebody to believe that everlasting life is possible and not tell them that?"[8] This entertainer who professed atheism could see that the man who gave him this Bible was actually living out his faith.

If I really believe that there is a real hell and a real heaven, and if I really believe that Jesus is the Lord, how much would I have to hate someone not to tell them that?

St. John Paul II pointed out that the opposite of love is not hatred; the opposite of love is use or indifference.[9] A lot of us would be quick to say that we don't hate anyone. But I think many of us are indifferent to others. Do we really believe that people are worth trying to save? What about the people who are closest to us?

A few years ago, I knew a college student I'll call Natalie. Natalie was part of the Catholic community on her campus, and her first year, second year, and third year, she kept growing and growing. She recognized that God had done amazing things for her. Then, in her senior year, she began to be a little resistant to the Lord as she looked ahead to what would happen after college.

During her senior year, she went to a youth conference run by FOCUS. She resisted going to this conference because she had gone before and felt like she didn't need to go there again. But in the end, she decided to go, and at that conference God opened her heart more deeply. God had already changed Natalie's life, but at this conference, Natalie was convinced that what God had done in her couldn't stop with her. Specifically, the Lord helped her grow in the love she has for her little brother and little sister.

If you have ever tried to share the Gospel with your siblings, you might have found out that it doesn't always work well. For Natalie, her little brother and sister were going off to college soon, and she said, "I want someone to be able to reach them." She decided, "There's someone else's little brother and little sister going off to college right now, and maybe I can be there for them, just as I hope someone will be there for my brother and sister."

Natalie saw a way to carry out the mission by becoming a FOCUS missionary. She did not want to let what Jesus did in her stop with her, and that is the call for all of us. But many of us may ask, "Where do we start?"

WHERE TO START

We are called to act, but where do we start? In Acts 1, before the Holy Spirit came upon the disciples with dynamite power, Jesus told them how to begin to be witnesses. He said, "You shall be my witnesses in Jerusalem and in all Judea and Samaria and to the end of the earth" (Acts 1:8). He told them to start right where they were in the city of Jerusalem.

Basically, Jesus says to us, "Start where you are." Just start at home. Start right now. So often we think, "Well, I'll have to go to Calcutta. I'll have to go to a distant country. I have to go to some other place." No. We can start where we are.

Where do we start? We can start right now where we are.

One of the mottos here at the Newman Center at UMD is "See a need, fill a need." It's not just a motto that gets people to vacuum the floor, although it's supposed to do that—it's a model that is meant to give us a vision for how to live. If I see a need, I want to fill a need.

If I see a need, that is where I can start to live the mission. If I see a need, maybe that is the call. If I see someone who is hungry, maybe I'm the person who can feed them. If I see someone who is lonely, maybe I can be the one to be a friend. If I see someone who does not know who Jesus is, maybe I can fill that need. The alternative is to live as if we don't have a call; or as if we have a call, but we don't have the gifts; or as if we have the call and have the gifts, but we don't use them.

The great call that Jesus Christ has extended to you and to me, the great call Jesus has extended to every single one of us, is to go make disciples. He has not left us alone. He has not left us powerless. He has given us the strength to do this.

We were not baptized to show up and just watch. Jesus Christ did not come to this earth and give us the gift of the Eucharist so we could just show up to Mass and watch. He did not die and rise from the dead and send his Holy Spirit into your life and my life so we could just show up and receive his gifts but never use them. He did those things so that we could unite our lives and our sacrifices to his life and his sacrifice. He has given us the power to accomplish the mission he has given us.

We pray that God stirs that strength, stirs those gifts, and stirs that power of the Holy Spirit into flame in our hearts so that we will come to the altar and then go out and live the mission of Jesus. We pray that when there is someone lonely, we'll be the one there; when there is someone hungry, we'll be the one there; when there is someone who doesn't know Jesus, we'll be the one there. Because I believe that none of us wants to allow what Jesus has done in us to stop with us.

REFLECT

Have you ever been given a mission or project that seemed impossible? How did you respond?

Jesus offers us salvation from sin through his sacrifice on the Cross, re-presented on the altar at Mass, and the Father has poured out the Holy Spirit upon the world. How have these gifts of God made a difference in your life?

Have you ever shared the Gospel with someone you knew did not believe? Was it a stranger or a friend or a family member? How did the other person respond?

What are some areas in your life where you see others' needs? Discuss ways you could fill those needs.

The greatest need for each person is salvation. Have you ever felt like you had to go "some other place" before you could start fulfilling the mission of evangelization? Discuss how you can begin to spread the Gospel right where you are.

PRAY

You have a very clear call to make disciples of Jesus in this world, but you do not have to fulfill this call in the exact same way as anyone else ever has! That is the beauty of having a relationship with God. He loves you uniquely, and you get the wonderful gift of sharing that singular relationship with the world around you.

As you begin your prayer time, let yourself be silent and allow the Holy Spirit to remind you of all the powerful things he has done in you. Think of all the times he has delivered you from fear. Think of the times he has comforted you in specific needs. Think of the times he has provided for you in your material needs. Allow him to do a play-by-play montage of his goodness in your life.

To close out your time with the Lord in prayer, ask him to show you how you can bring his goodness into the world. Ask him to show you the family, friends, and strangers around you who might need to be delivered from fear, comforted in need, provided for materially, and told the Good News of Christ. When God brings something or someone to mind, resolve to act upon it. Decide to "go into all the world" with the power and presence of God. Resolve that what he has done in you will not stop with you.

ACT ///

For the rest of this day, be alert for the needs of others and for ways that you can fill those needs so that what God has done in you will not stop with you today.

REMEMBER

- The heart of religion is worship—and the heart of worship is sacrifice. We need to come to the altar of the Lord and worship, regardless of how we are feeling, because this is how we love God.

- The Mass is the sacrifice of Jesus on the Cross re-presented on the altar. In the Mass, we behold God's love for us and then receive this love in the Body, Blood, Soul, and Divinity of his Son.

- Every baptized Christian participates in the "common priesthood of all the faithful" (CCC 1547). At Mass, we are called to unite our hearts to the sacrifice of Jesus.

- Giving our firstfruits to the Lord both reveals and increases our trust in him. This helps us to stop watching and start worshipping at Mass; we make his sacrifice ours as we come to the altar.

- God has given us the mission of spreading the Gospel, and he has given us the power to live out that mission so that what he has done in us will not stop with us.

NOTES

1. Mark M. Gray, ed., "Where Is Mass Attendance Highest and Lowest?," *Center for Applied Research in the Apostolate*, cara.georgetown.edu. These numbers are from a poll of Catholics in late summer 2022 who said they attended Mass at least once every week.

2. Jackie and Bobby Angel, "Did Early Christians Believe in the Eucharist?," *Ascension Presents*, YouTube video, June 16, 2022, media.ascensionpress.com.

3. See St. Augustine, *Tractates (Lectures) on the Gospel of John* 5.18, newadvent.org.

4. Fulton J. Sheen, *The Priest Is Not His Own* (New York: McGraw-Hill, 1963), 9.

5. Uri Friedman, "How an Ad Campaign Invented the Diamond Engagement Ring," *The Atlantic* (February 13, 2015), theatlantic.com.

6. See Rev. William Saunders, "The Magi," reprinted with permission from *Arlington Catholic Herald*, 2003, Catholic Education Resource Center, catholiceducation.org, accessed July 31, 2023.

7. See "The Cross Exemplifies Every Virtue," from a conference by St. Thomas Aquinas (Collatio 6 super *Credo in Deum*), liturgies.net.

8. Erin Roach, "Atheism: Penn Jillette Urges Evangelism," Baptist Press, February 12, 2009, baptistpress.com.

9. See Edward Sri, "Love and Responsibility: Beyond the Sexual Urge," reprinted with permission from *Lay Witness*, March/April 2005, Catholic Education Resource Center, catholiceducation.org, accessed July 26, 2023.